21st Century Skills Library

21st
Century
Skills Library

COOL MILITARY CAREERS

DRONE PILOT

NANCY ROBINSON MASTERS

CHERRY
LAKE
Publishing

Published in the United States of America by
Cherry Lake Publishing, Ann Arbor, Michigan
www.cherrylakepublishing.com

Content Adviser
Cynthia Watson, PhD, author of *U.S. National Security*

Credits
Cover and pages 1 and 26, U.S. Air Force photo by Staff Sgt. Donald R. Allen/Released;
page 4, U.S. Navy photo by Mass Communication Specialist 2nd Class Joseph M. Buliavac/
Released; page 6, U.S. Marine Corps photo by Cpl. Richard A. Tetreau/Released; page 8,
U.S. Air Force photo by Tech. Sgt. Erik Gudmundson/Released; page 9, U.S. Army photo by
Staff Sgt. Kyle Richardson/Released; page 11, U.S. Navy photo by Mass Communication
Specialist 2nd Class Alan Gragg/Released; page 12, U.S. Air Force photo by Rich
McFadden/Released; page 14, U.S. Air Force photo by Senior Airman Brett Clashman/
Released; pages 16, 22, and 27, DoD photo by Val Gempis, U.S. Air Force/Released;
page 18, U.S. Army photo by Spc. Rosalind Arroyo/Released; page 20, U.S. Air Force
photo by Tech. Sgt. James Harper/Released; page 24, U.S. Marine Corps photo by Lance
Cpl. Michael C. Nerl/Released; page 29, U.S. Army photo by Spc. Roland Hale/Released

Library of Congress Cataloging-in-Publication Data
Masters, Nancy Robinson.
 Drone pilot/by Nancy Robinson Masters.
    p. cm.—(Cool military careers)
 Includes bibliographical references and index.
 Audience: Grades 4–6.
 ISBN 978-1-61080-448-6 (lib. bdg.) — ISBN 978-1-61080-535-3 (e-book) —
ISBN 978-1-61080-622-0 (pbk.)
 1. Drone aircraft—United States—Juvenile literature. 2. Air pilots, Military—
United States—Juvenile literature. 3. United States—Armed Forces—Vocational
guidance—Juvenile literature.
 UG1242.D7M36 2012
 358.4—dc23   2012010756

Cherry Lake Publishing would like to acknowledge
the work of The Partnership for 21st Century Skills.
Please visit *www.21stcenturyskills.org* for more information.

Printed in the United States of America
Corporate Graphics Inc.
July 2012
CLFA11

TABLE OF CONTENTS

CHAPTER ONE
WHAT ARE DRONES?

"**Z**ack! Look at this!"

Cassie clicked the computer mouse. A video began playing on the monitor. The video showed a swarm of 16 robots that

Unmanned aerial vehicles are much smaller than aircraft that are built to hold pilots.

looked like tiny helicopters. They were flying inside a gymnasium. Each was about the size of a large dinner plate. Four small, whirling rotary blades provided lift as they flew through the air.

"Wow! Is this a new science-fiction movie?" Zack asked. He and his sister were huge sci-fi fans.

"No, this is even better. This is a video made at a scientific research facility," Cassie said. "These are **remotely** piloted aircraft being tested for future military use. This video demonstrates how one military pilot may be able to fly 16 aircraft at the same time without them crashing into each other."

Zack took a deep breath. He had wanted to be a military pilot since he began flying remote-controlled model aircraft. It would be awesome to be the pilot of 16 aircraft flying at the same time!

"On an actual mission, the pilot might be thousands of miles away," Cassie said. "Or the pilot could be flying in an aircraft while also controlling a group of unmanned aircraft. That's what a **drone** pilot does. That would be a cool military career for you, Zack."

Zack smiled. It would be a cool military career for his sister, too!

■ ■ ■

Drones are unmanned aerial vehicles (UAVs). Military pilots usually refer to them as remotely piloted aircraft (RPA).

They are the "eyes in the skies" for the troops on the ground. Drones are the fastest-growing type of airplane being developed and used by the United States military. In the near future, they will be as important as combat pilots in the country's armed forces.

Drones are used for **intelligence** flights to gather secret information, for **surveillance** flights to observe what is

UAVs can operate in combat areas while their pilots are in less dangerous locations.

happening on the ground, and for **reconnaissance** flights to explore unknown or unsafe areas. Drones armed with missiles and bombs are used to attack targets in combat zones. Almost one out of every three aircraft used by the U.S. military is a drone.

 LIFE & CAREER SKILLS

Not all drone pilots work in the military. Some work for government agencies, state and local governments, and large businesses. In these jobs, becoming a UAV pilot is similar to becoming an airline pilot. If you want to start out earning a high salary, you'll need a four-year college degree in engineering or aeronautics. Some people attend a college that offers a four-year degree and pilot training programs together. Doing that, you'll earn your degree and enough flight hours to qualify for an entry-level remotely piloted aircraft job. Whether you go to college or not, you'll need to earn a pilot license and log at least 500 hours of pilot-in-command flight hours.

Drones range in size from those with wingspans of less than 3 feet (0.9 meters) to the RQ-11B Raven with a wingspan of 4.5 feet (1.4 m) to the MQ-9 Reaper, which has a 66-foot (20.1 m) wingspan. The RQ-11B Raven weighs only 4 pounds (1.8 kilograms) and can be hand-launched by a person on the ground. The MQ-1 Predator, one of the most widely used drones, is 27 feet (8.2 m) long and has a wingspan of 48.7 feet (14.8 m). A helium-filled spy balloon equipped with a camera

The MQ-9 Reaper can carry up to 3,750 pounds (1701 kg) of bombs and missiles.

The RQ-11B Raven is extremely small and lightweight.

is the largest drone. This blimp is held to the ground by cables and floats 15,000 feet (4,572 m) in the air.

Some drones can be used for multiple purposes. Reapers can be used for spying and for attacking targets with weapons. The QF-4 drone is an F-4 Phantom jet that has been converted to a dual-purpose drone that flys at 1,600 miles (2,575 kilometers) an hour. It can be flown unmanned for missile target practice, or it can be flown with a pilot on board to teach combat maneuvers to pilots in other aircraft.

The U.S. Air Force flies more drones than any other branch of the military, but it is not the only branch that uses RPAs. The U.S. Navy uses the MQ-8B Fire Scout helicopter and is testing the experimental X-47B unmanned combat aircraft. The X-47B will take off from and land on **aircraft carriers**, and will be controlled only by onboard computer systems. The Navy is also testing drones that can travel underwater like submarines.

The U.S. Army and Marine Corps use the RQ-7 Shadow for reconnaissance missions. The Grey Eagle drone assigned to the Army Combat Aircraft Brigade is similar to the Air Force Predator drone. Other government agencies, such as the Central Intelligence Agency (CIA), the organization responsible for providing national security intelligence to U.S. leaders, also use drones.

The MQ-8B Fire Scout is often used for reconnaissance missions.

CHAPTER TWO
TRAINING TO BE A DRONE PILOT

J oining the armed forces is a life-changing deci-
sion, so think carefully before you make the move. Give

Pilots learn about all of their UAVs capabilities during training.

much thought as to why you want to join. Is it to get a job? Perhaps you want to serve your country? Is it to learn a trade? Are you looking for adventure and excitement? Whatever your reasons, speak with your family to get their support. You can also speak with a military **recruiter**, who will be able to give you all the details about serving in the U.S. armed forces. Each branch of the military has its own knowledgeable recruiters.

You must be a member of the Army, Navy, Air Force, Marines or Coast Guard before you can fly military drones. You may be assigned to a drone squadron, or you may apply to fly drones after you complete basic training in the branch of the military you join. Both men and women are permitted to be drone pilots.

The first drone pilots were experienced combat or support aircraft pilots. The Air Force has recently developed a training program that teaches members of the military who have never flown an airplane to be a drone pilot. Today, the Air Force trains more drone pilots than it trains pilots of manned bombers and fighters combined. It also trains more drone pilots than any other branch of the military.

Competition for drone pilot training among nonpilots in the military is fierce. However, not many experienced combat or support aircraft pilots apply for drone positions. They prefer to fly manned aircraft.

The plan for training RPA pilots to become full professionals is called the drone pipeline. If you are already a military pilot, you begin the pipeline by attending the RPA qualification course. Here you train on **simulators** to learn computer and communication skills that are unique to flying drones. This is followed by a course to learn military **tactics** for conducting drone missions.

If you are selected for drone pilot training but are not already a military pilot, your first step on the pipeline will be

Drone pilots must train to fly manned aircraft before flying drones.

to log several hours of actual flight training in an airplane. You will do this before you begin the RPA qualification course.

Drone pilots must pass physical requirements just like pilots who fly manned aircraft. Good vision is necessary, although a drone pilot's vision does not need to be as good as that of a fighter pilot. Here's a brief look at the five skills you'll need to be a successful drone pilot:

Dedicated

Responsible

Organized

Never out of control

Eager to get the job done right

Student drone pilots and **sensor** operators begin working together for the first time during advanced drone flight training. Most of this training is conducted at Holloman Air Force Base in New Mexico and at Creech Air Force Base in Nevada. The pilot and sensor operator sit side by side at a workstation in a simulator bay, which is a small room that contains computer processors and monitors. Their workstation is a copy of the Predator drone's cockpit.

An instructor puts up images of a foreign combat zone on their computer screens. He tells the pilot and sensor operator trainees that they are to simulate flying a drone under combat conditions. The students train in long shifts, learning to use top-secret computer programs and equipment. They also learn to manage their levels of fatigue and stress, and to deal with periods of boredom that are a part of some drone missions.

After mastering the simulator, the trainees are assigned to ground control stations on the **tarmac** of the Air Force base runway. Sitting in large, rectangular, metal storage containers, the students actually control real Predators and Reapers on test runs. After their shift, another team comes in to relieve them.

Pilots get experience controlling UAVs during their time at ground control stations.

LEARNING & INNOVATION SKILLS

Drone sensors are systems built into RPAs to collect and store intelligence and reconnaissance information. Sensor operators work alongside drone pilots and assist in preflight and in-flight planning activities and navigation. They also research and study target imagery, monitor drone weapons systems, and assemble information about enemy forces. They often determine possible tactics for their RPAs to take. Sensor operators must think fast and react promptly to information being provided by the drone sensors. A student training to be a sensor operator is often paired with an RPA pilot trainee, and they attend a course together as a two-person flight team.

Pilots graduate from advanced training ready to operate Predator and Reaper drones. They have the skills necessary to learn to fly other kinds of drones as well, but they must be flexible and able to adapt quickly to changing technology.

CHAPTER THREE
FLYING A DRONE

Since the September 11, 2001, terrorist attacks on the United States, the number of drones used by the U.S. military has increased from 60 to about 6,000. Drones are ideal weapons when fighting enemies in distant nations such as Iraq, Afghanistan, and Pakistan. They can

Drones have played a major role in recent combat operations in Afghanistan.

stay in the air for 24 hours or longer, and they have the ability to track and attack enemies while keeping U.S. forces out of harm's way.

Amazingly, a drone pilot at a command center in the United States can safely control a drone launched from a location thousands of miles away. In some cases, the drone pilot may be working from a ground control room close to the target area. In either case, drone technology is changing the way wars are being fought.

 LIFE & CAREER SKILLS

Do you like to play video games? The USAF 558th Training Squadron at Randolph Air Force Base in San Antonio, Texas, has a goal of training 180 drone pilots each year. Some of the pilots in training come from other branches of the military. Others come from countries that are working with the United States against a common threat. "One of the first things all drone pilots learn is that flying a military drone is not the same thing as playing a video game on a computer," the squadron commander explains. "However, some of the skills used to play computer games can be helpful when learning to be a drone pilot." What computer game skills do you think would be helpful for a drone pilot to have?

Two of the most widely used drones in Afghanistan and Pakistan are the medium-size Predator and Reaper. These odd-looking crafts can be equipped with television cameras, infrared sighting devices used for low-light conditions, and lasers for targeting. Both types of drones can be fitted with deadly laser-guided bombs and missiles.

Drone operators close to the location of the mission handle drone takeoffs and landings. Once the drone is airborne, military drone pilots, usually located at an airbase in

Predator drones allow their pilots to see deep into enemy territory.

the United States, take over the flight activities—thousands of miles away from the action. Bouncing commands off a satellite link orbiting high above Earth, the pilot and sensor operator guide the drone to its target to carry out its mission. The pilot relies on cameras inside the drone to see what's going on around the craft. The drone is also capable of transmitting data and images to ground troops near the target. They make decisions about controlling the drone based on the information they receive.

Being a drone pilot puts you on the "virtual" front lines of war. With your bank of computer screens and control devices at hand, you can see a battle unfold in front of you from far away. Captain Alex is one such "virtual" soldier. He is a member of the Air Force who has been a drone pilot for two years. Like other active-duty drone pilots, Captain Alex identifies himself only by his **rank** and first name while he is working a drone mission.

Captain Alex works with a combat air patrol unit based in a secret location near a war zone. Their missions include using a Predator drone to track the movements of suspected terrorists. Alex uses a keyboard and a control stick like those used by fighter pilots to control the drone circling 30,000 feet (9,144 m) above a remote mountain area in Afghanistan.

Alex begins his day with a briefing with other team members. He works an eight-hour shift in a darkened room lit only by the glow of light from flat computer screens. The room is underground at a drone command center far from the battle-field. While on duty, he wears an Air Force flight suit. He earns flight pay in addition to his regular Air Force salary.

Unlike flying a manned aircraft, there is no feeling of thrust or pull of gravity when he moves the controls. The clos-est Alex has ever been to an actual manned fighter or bomber

In some ways, controlling a drone is similar to playing a video game.

aircraft was while he was in training to fly drones. "Our work-station was next to a runway where B-1 bombers landed to refuel," he said. "Everything shook when a B-1 took off, including us!"

The sensor operator seated next to Alex relays information received from the drone sensors and from members of the combat air patrol team on the ground where the Predator is based. These crew members are responsible for maintaining the Predator that Alex flies. "When people ask me what I do, I tell them I am a pilot. When they ask me what I fly, I just smile and tell them I fly airplanes," Alex says. "That's all."

CHAPTER FOUR
DRONE PILOTS IN THE FUTURE

Acareer as a drone pilot will be very different in the future. New technology will allow machines to perform

More and more missions are being flown by UAVs instead of manned aircraft.

jobs that now require human intelligence. For example, a test program is under way to allow the Global Hawk drone—with its 17,300-gallon (65,488-liter) fuel capacity—to refuel another Global Hawk drone in the air using only computer instructions and responses. Some military career planners think human hands will never touch the controls of drones during military operations in the future. Other career planners believe human pilots will always be needed.

21ST CENTURY CONTENT

Drones were originally designed to be a "flying pair of binoculars." But U.S. military leaders saw the potential to use them as offensive weapons, and drones were eventually built to carry weapons. Future uses of military drones include carrying cargo and delivering medical supplies and equipment to remote locations. The drones will be able to drop their loads at a prearranged spot, or on directions from the ground, and then return to their home bases. The UAVs will be able to land automatically or by remote control.

The U.S. military is currently fine-tuning a helicopter-style drone that can take off straight up, meaning that runways will not be needed. The new craft, the A160 Hummingbird, will also be able to **hover**. It will be equipped with video equipment that is strong enough to track vehicles and people from heights of more than 20,000 feet (6,096 m) across almost 65 square miles (168 sq km).

Drones are sure to play an important role in the U.S. military in the future.

New technology will make UAVs even more useful.

Smaller drone designs are being developed for use in the 21st century. Researchers and scientists at a laboratory at Wright-Patterson Air Force Base in Ohio are experimenting with drones that can imitate the flight of moths and hawks. They are also working to shrink drones that can spy and strike to the size of insects. By 2030, the U.S. military hopes to have swarms of these "spy flies" operating.

As technology advances and the U.S. military comes to rely more on UAVs, the future for drone pilots looks to be busy. The Air Force's current staff of about 350 drone pilots and their support crews have been pushed to their limits. The search is on for competent, highly qualified men and women to step up and take the controls of this cutting-edge technology. Do you have the right stuff to make a difference in the U.S. military?

Will you become a drone pilot one day?

GLOSSARY

aircraft carriers (AIR-kraft KAR-ee-urz) warships with a large, flat deck where aircraft take off and land

drone (DROHN) an unmanned aerial vehicle that is controlled remotely

hover (HUHV-ur) to remain in one place in the air

intelligence (in-TEL-uh-juhnts) information gathered and used by government agencies to plan and make important decisions

rank (RANGK) official job level or position

reconnaissance (ri-KON-uh-zuhnts) a survey of an area to gather information

recruiter (ri-KROO-tur) a military employee in charge of signing up new members and providing information to people who are interested in joining the military

remotely (ri-MOHT-lee) from far away

sensor (SEN-suhr) instrument that can detect and measure changes and transmit the information to a controlling device

simulators (SIM-yuh-lay-turz) machines that allow you to perform a task, such as flying a plane, by imitating the conditions and controls

surveillance (sur-VAY-luntz) close observation of a person or group

tactics (TAK-tiks) plans or methods to win a battle

tarmac (TAR-mak) the area of an airfield where craft take off and land

FOR MORE INFORMATION

BOOKS

Hamilton, John. *UAVs: Unmanned Aerial Vehicles*. Minneapolis, MN: ABDO, 2012.

Yenne, Bill. *Birds of Prey: Predators, Reapers and America's Newest UAVs in Combat*. North Branch, MN: Specialty Press, 2010.

WEB SITES

Aviation Schools Online—UAV and UAS Pilot & Sensor Operator Careers
www.aviationschoolsonline.com/faqs/uav-pilot-careers.php
Learn more about drone pilots, sensor operators, and schools that provide training for future UAV workers.

U.S. Air Force
www.airforce.com
Check out this site to learn more about careers, benefits, and life in the Air Force, as well as see exciting videos of high-flying Air Force action.

INDEX

ABOUT THE AUTHOR

Nancy Robinson Masters is an airplane pilot who has written dozens of books and more than 3,000 feature stories about airplanes and aviation. She presents visiting author programs at schools and was named the Distinguished Citizen of the Year by the U.S. Air Force in recognition of her patriotic support of American air power and the freedom of free people to read and write. Nancy and her husband, veteran aviator Bill Masters, live in the Elmdale Community near Abilene, Texas.